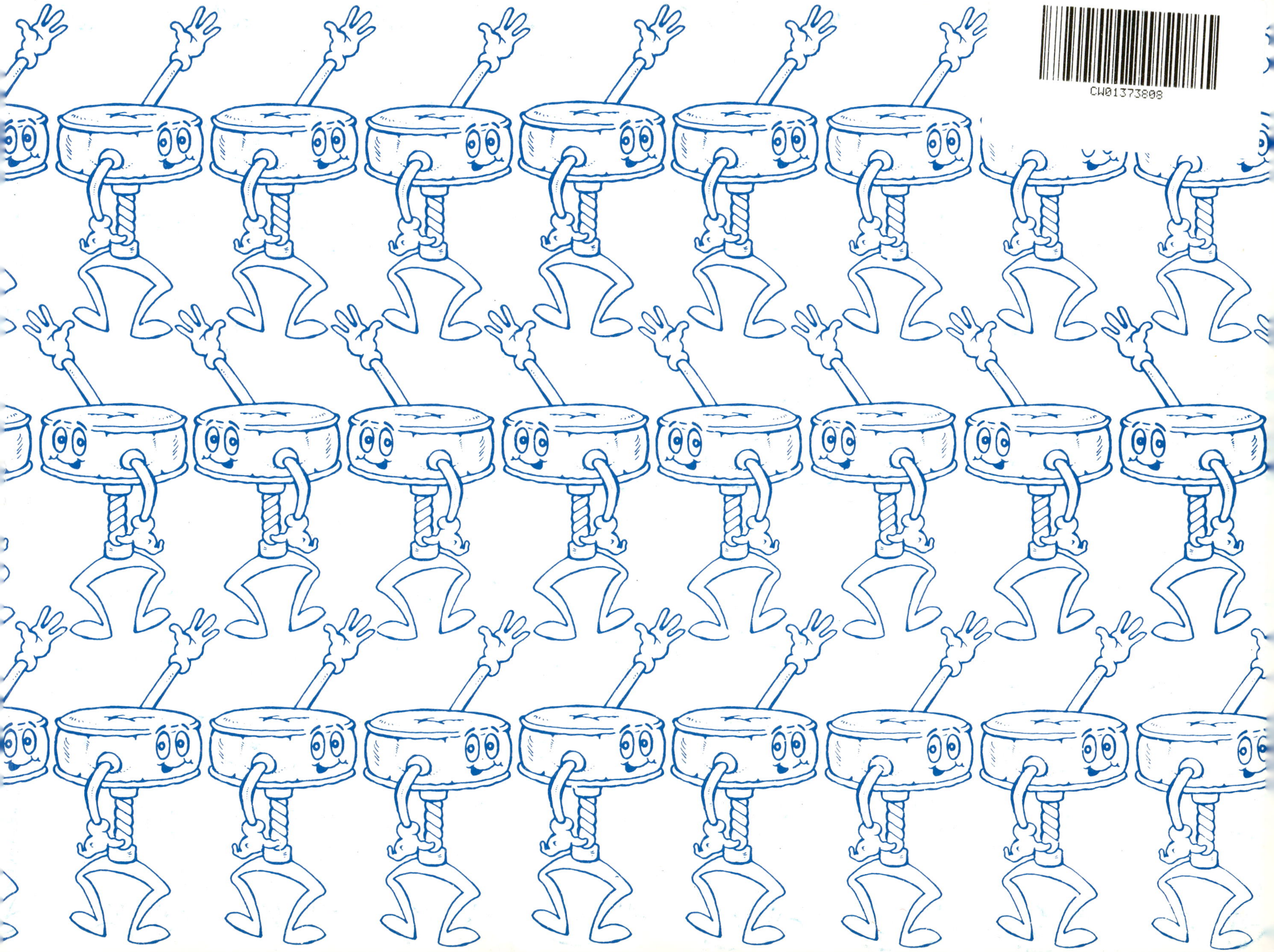

First published 1983
Published by Hamish Hamilton Children's Books
Garden House, 57–59 Long Acre, London WC2E 9JZ

Produced for Hamish Hamilton Children's Books by
Victoria House Publishing, Paulton, Bristol BS18 5LQ
Text and music Copyright © 1983
Chappell Music Limited
Design and illustrations Copyright © 1983
Victoria House Publishing

Design and illustrations by Graham Brown
and Michael Wells of Brown, Wells, Jacobs Ltd.
All Rights Reserved
Made and Printed in Gt. Britain by Purnell & Sons
(Book Production) Ltd., Paulton (Bristol) and London

ISBN 0 241 10978 7

THE CHAPPELL PIANO BOOK

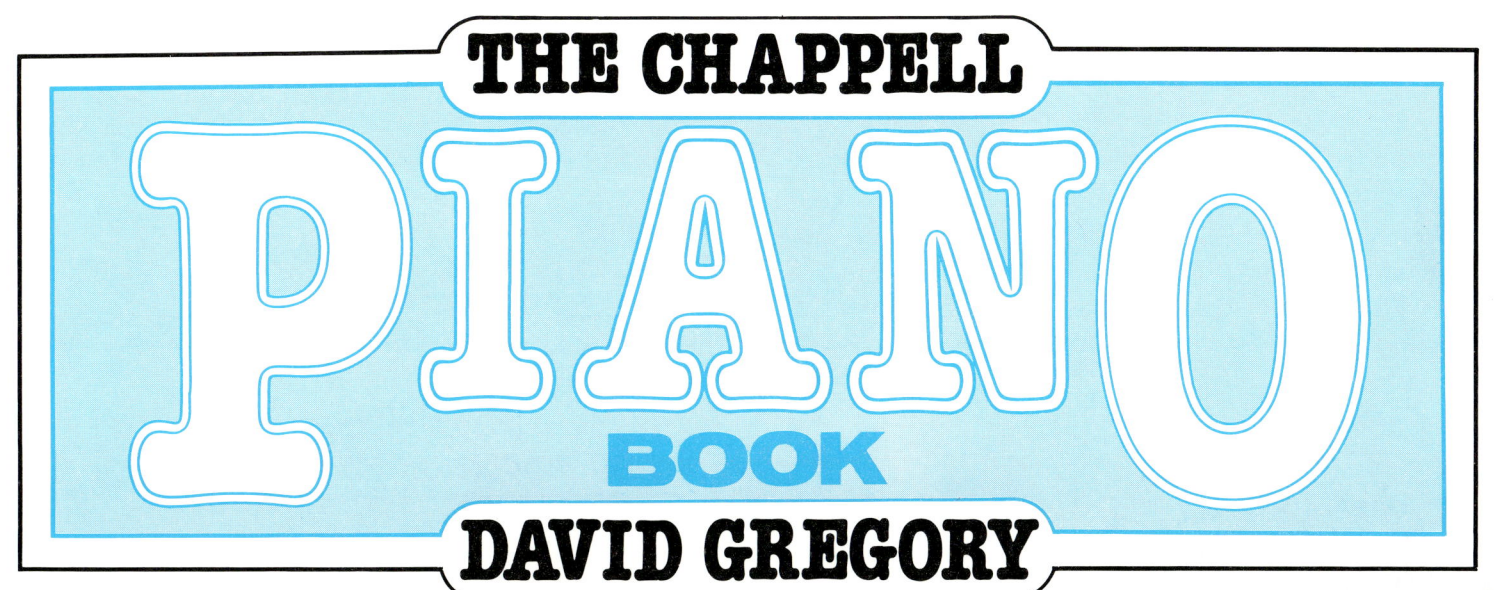

DAVID GREGORY

Hamish Hamilton London

CONTENTS

Introduction	3	Eighth Note – Quaver	24
Your Piano	4	Rests	26
How to Begin	6	Phrases	28
The Musical Alphabet	8	A New Note – F sharp	30
Playing from Music	10	A New Note – B flat	32
Playing Middle C	11	Time for Music	34
Up and Down from Middle C	12	More New Notes – Left Hand	36
Bar Lines and Measures	14	More New Notes – Right Hand	37
Changing the Beat	15	Playing a Scale – Left Hand	40
Whole Note – Semibreve	16	Playing a Scale – Right Hand	42
Half Note – Minim	17	Tunes to Play	19, 25, 27, 29, 31, 33, 35, 38, 39, 41, 43, 44, 45, 46, 47, 48
Quarter Note – Crotchet	18		
Two New Notes – Left Hand	20		
Two New Notes – Right Hand	21		
Hands Together	22		
Dotted Half Note	23		

Hello!

So you want to play the piano. I know every piano in the world – yes, even yours and in this book I will tell you everything you need to know about your piano and how to play it.

I have written new music specially for you and included a part for your teacher to add to the fun.

I've had a great time appearing in this book. I hope you enjoy it too. When you finish you will know all about the notes and the music you can make on your piano. I'll be popping up to help you along the way, so follow me and soon you'll be able to play all your favourite tunes.

YOUR PIANO

There are two main types of piano. Some are very big **GRAND** pianos, and some are smaller **UPRIGHT** pianos. Which is yours?

Sit down in front of your piano and open the lid. These are the keys. Some are black and some are white.

Press one of the keys. What happened? You made a **SOUND**. The sound is called a **NOTE**.

This is my **UPRIGHT** piano. If you have a different kind of piano don't worry, they all play in the same way.

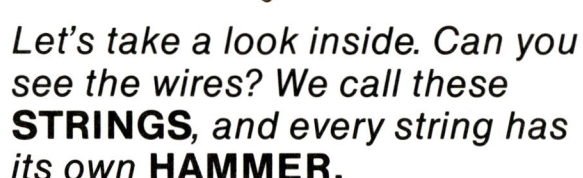

Let's take a look inside. Can you see the wires? We call these **STRINGS**, and every string has its own **HAMMER**.

String → ← **Hammer**

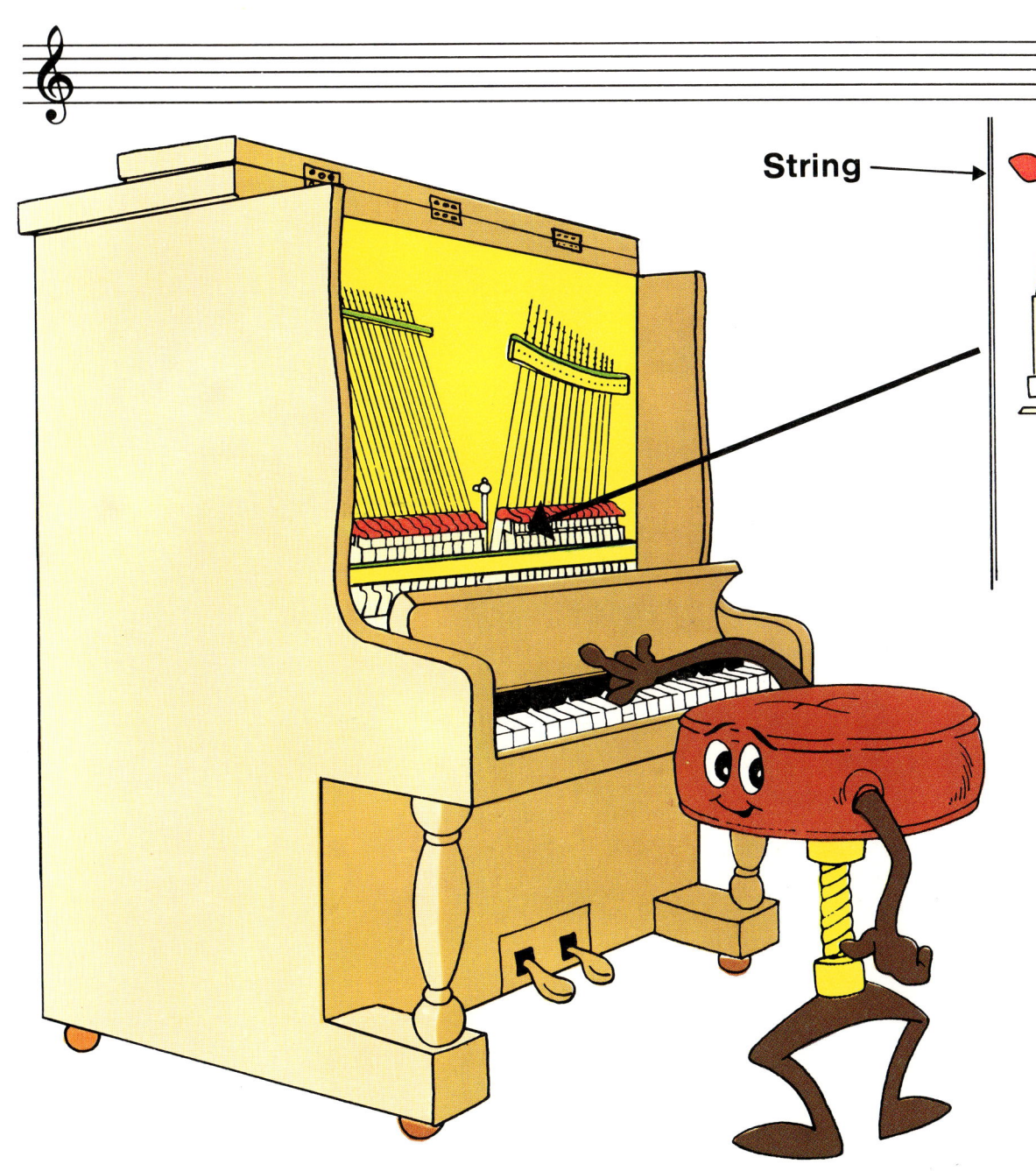

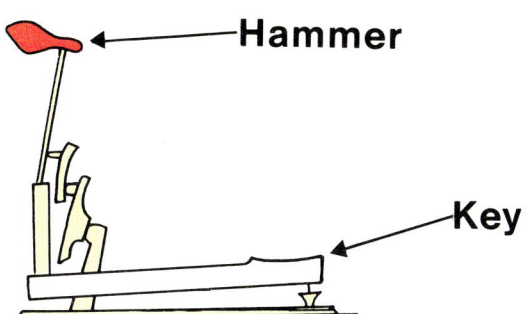

← **Key**

Press a key and watch what happens. Did you see the hammer hit the string?

Some of the strings are big thick strings. Press a key and hit a thick string. These make 'low, deep' sounds.

Other strings are thin. Press a key and hit a thin string. These make 'high, bright' sounds.

Press the key slowly and the note will play soft. Press the key quickly and the note will be loud. Play some loud and soft, high and low notes.

HOW TO BEGIN

Now we're ready to play. First we have to sit properly. Sit comfortably on the piano stool with both feet on the ground. Now drop your hands down by your side and let them relax.

If your hands are very relaxed your fingers will curve as though you are holding a ball, this is how they should be when you begin to play.

Gently bring your hands up to the keys and let them rest.

Your fingers should be curved so the tips of your fingers rest on the keys.

Do you know which is your left hand? And which is your right hand? Play some notes with your left hand and then some notes with your right hand.

Can you hear the notes played with your left hand are low deep sounds, and notes played with your right hand are high bright sounds?

HIGH

The more to the left or 'bottom' of the piano you play the 'lower' the notes become.

The more to the right or 'top' of the piano you play the 'higher' the notes become.

LOW

Play some high and low notes. Before you begin make sure you are sitting properly with your hands down by your side and your fingers curved.

THE MUSICAL ALPHABET

Musical notes are named after the first seven letters of the alphabet. **A B C D E F G.** If you look at your piano you will see far more notes than just seven – what do you think happens when we run out of letters?

We just start all over again at A.

Look at your piano again. Can you see that the black keys are in groups of two and three? Point to all the groups of two black keys and then all the groups of three.

Find the group of two black keys nearest to the middle of the piano. Play the white key just to the left. This note is called **C**.

All the other C's on your piano will be in the same place to the left of a group of two black keys.

The C in the middle has a special name. It is called **MIDDLE C.**

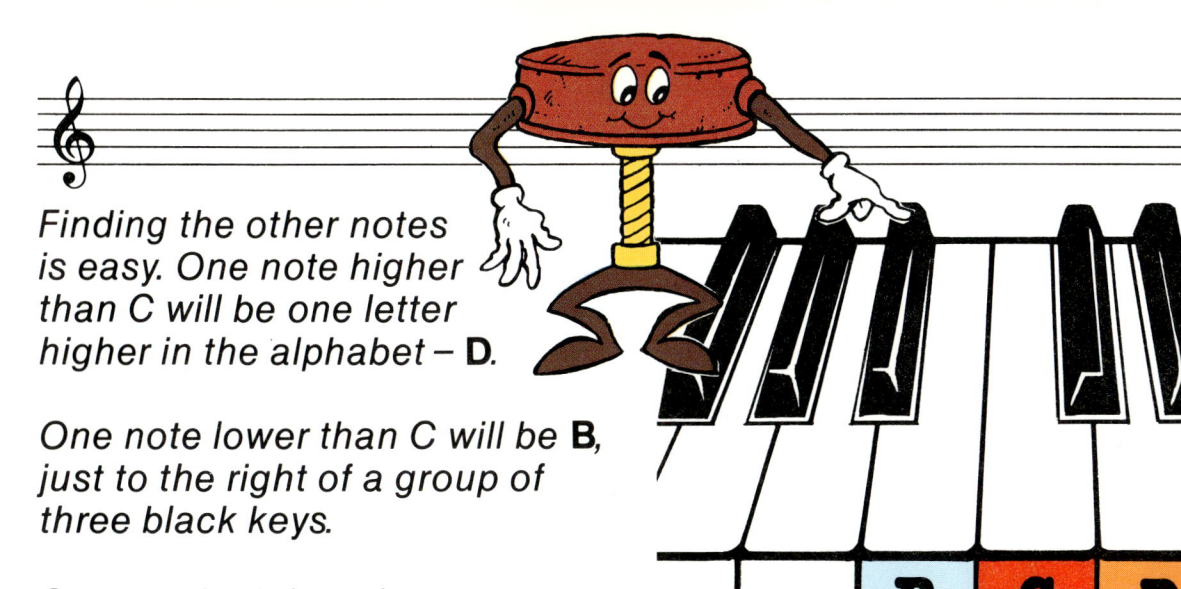

Finding the other notes is easy. One note higher than C will be one letter higher in the alphabet – **D**.

One note lower than C will be **B**, just to the right of a group of three black keys.

Can you find the other notes on your own?

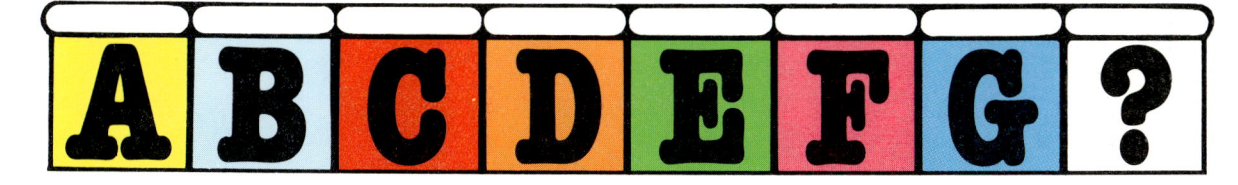

Now you can play the whole musical alphabet. Start at A and work up.

Do you know what note follows G?

Just start again at A.

Play the A nearest the middle of the keyboard and then the next A to the right. Can you hear the difference in sound?

One is **HIGH** and one is **LOW**.

The distance from one letter name to the same one higher or lower is called an **OCTAVE.**

There are eight notes in an octave – **ABCDEFGA.**

THINGS TO DO

Practise playing all the A's from the bottom of the keyboard to the top. Then do the same for all the other notes. Use your left hand for low notes and your right hand for high ones. Use your left hand or your right hand in the middle. Try to bounce from one note to the next, just like a bouncing ball. Then you are 'jumping the octave'.

Copy the picture of the keyboard and write in the name of the notes. Colour them if you like.

Make up words using only the letters of the musical alphabet and then play the words. I'll start you off, **B A G.**

PLAYING FROM MUSIC

Now that you can find the notes on your piano, let's find them on the music.

This is a picture of a piece of music by a famous composer called Beethoven.

Allegretto (♩ = 120)

Notes are written on **lines** and in the **spaces** between the lines.

Point to some notes written on lines and some written in the spaces. The lines and spaces are called the **STAVE**.

Have you noticed the two signs at the beginning of the Stave?

The **BASS CLEF** usually tells us to play with the left hand. Notes **below** Middle C.

The **TREBLE CLEF** usually tells us to play with the right hand. Notes **above** Middle C.

Left (Bass Clef)

Right (Treble Clef)

PLAYING MIDDLE C

Middle C has a special place in the middle of the Stave on its own line.

Middle C can move around in its own space. When it is nearer the Treble Clef it is played with your **right hand**. When it is nearer the Bass Clef it is played with your **left hand**. If it is in the middle, you can choose which hand to use.

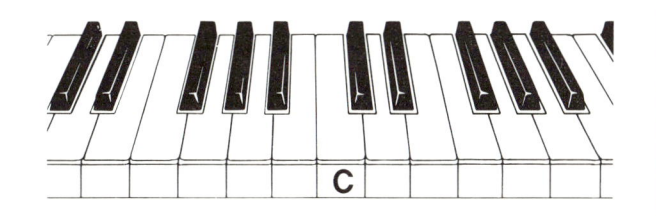

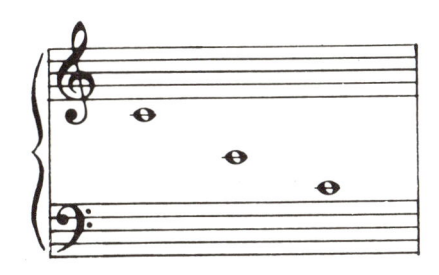

YOUR FIRST TUNE

Say the rhythm of the words before you play. Play each note using your thumb.

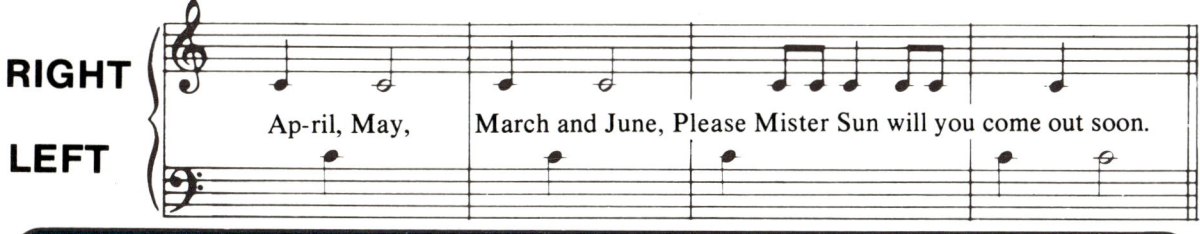

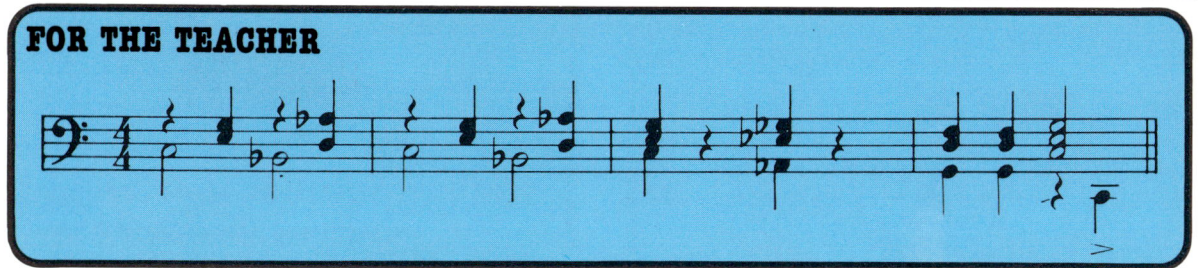

RIGHT

LEFT

Ap-ril, May, March and June, Please Mister Sun will you come out soon.

FOR THE TEACHER

THINGS TO DO

First draw the five lines.

Try drawing a Treble Clef like this

Try drawing a Bass Clef.

Draw the whole Stave with Middle C on its own line.

UP AND DOWN FROM MIDDLE C

One note **higher** than Middle C is **D**.

D is written in the space **above** Middle C.

One note **lower** than Middle C is **B**.

B is written in the space **below** Middle C.

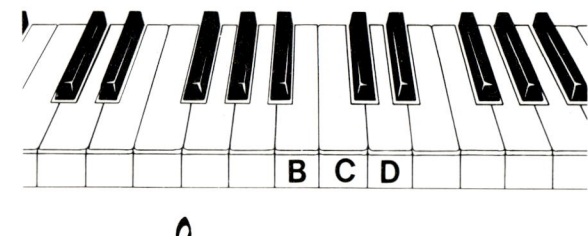

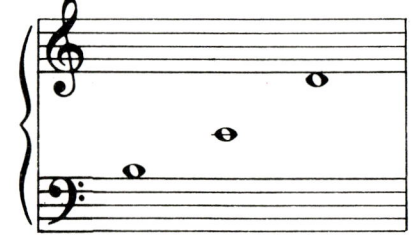

Play this music but first say and clap the rhythm of the words.

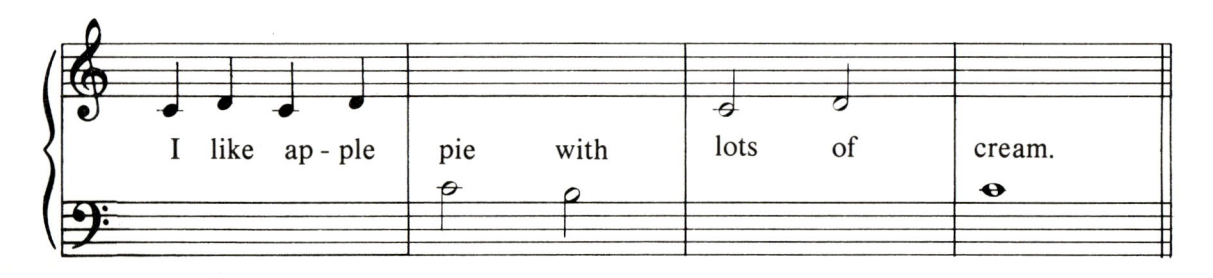

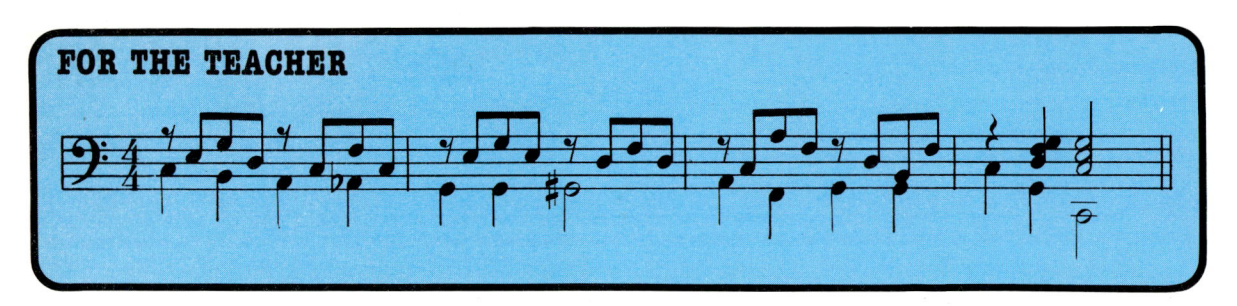

I like ap-ple pie with lots of cream.

FOR THE TEACHER

Which is your left hand?

Draw round your left hand and number the fingers.

Which is the first finger of your left hand?

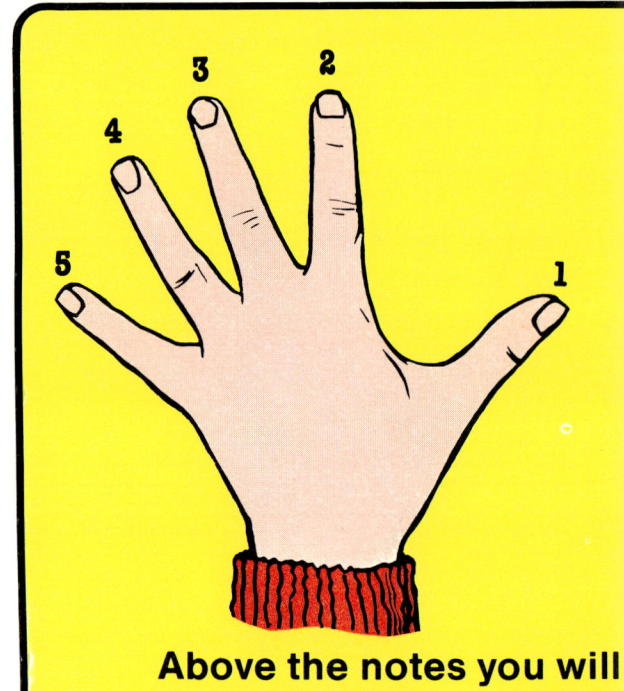

Above the notes you will This number tells us which noticed that we call the

Which is your right hand?

Draw round your right hand and number the fingers.

Which is the first finger of your right hand?

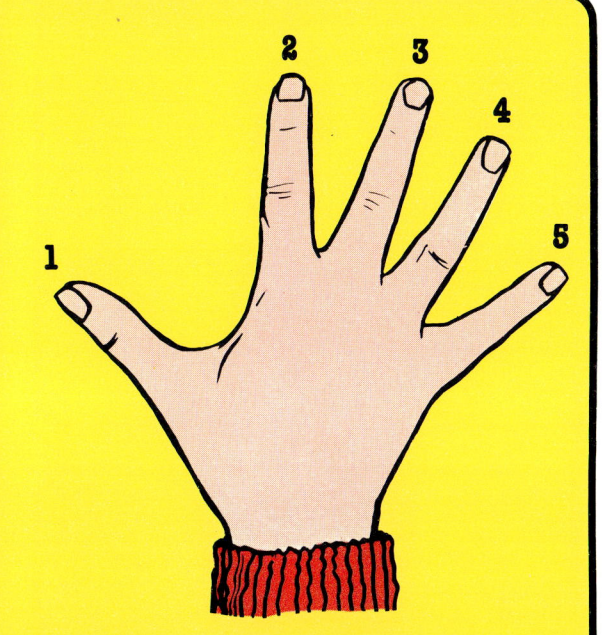

sometimes see a number. finger to play with. Have you thumb the first finger?

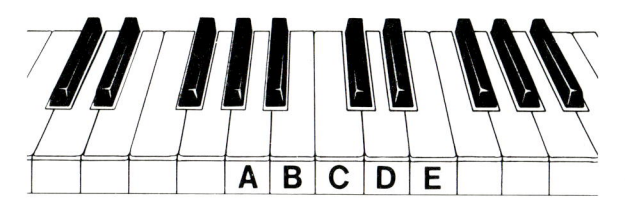

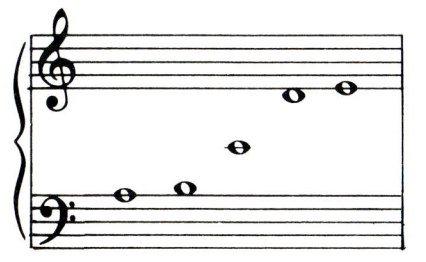

Two notes **higher** than Middle C will be **E**.

E is written on the first line of the Treble Clef.

Two notes **lower** than Middle C will be **A**.

A is written on the top line of the Bass Clef.

Play this music but first say and clap the rhythm of the words.

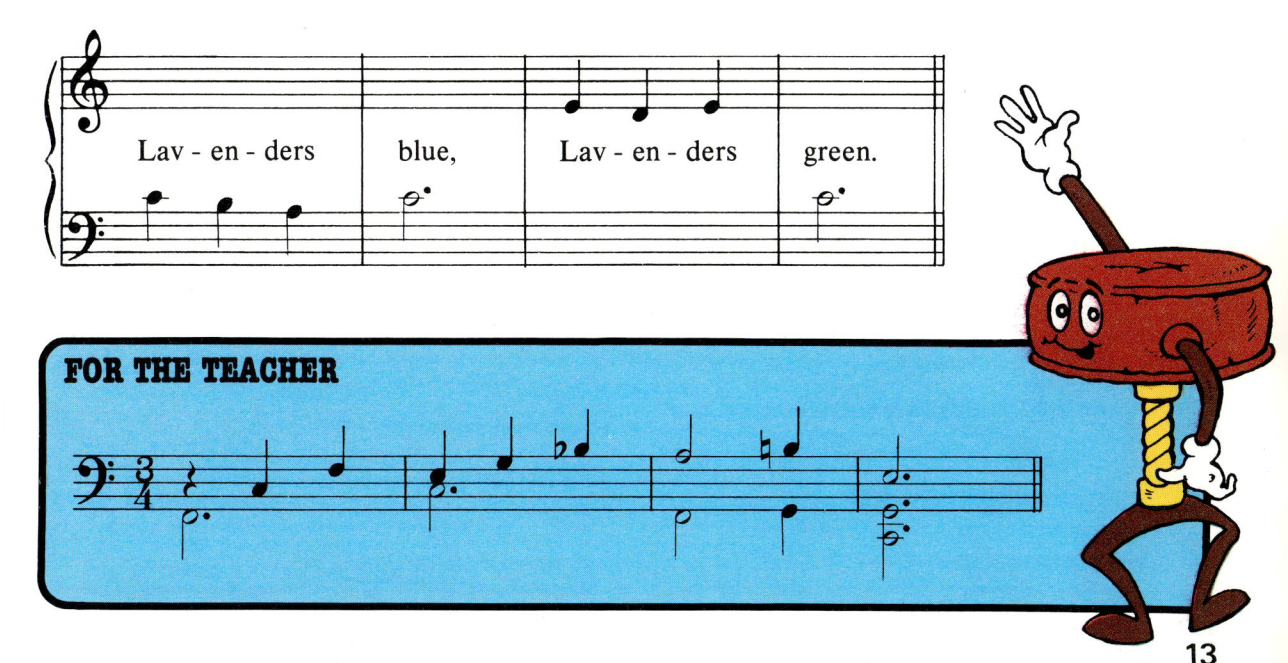

Lav - en - ders   blue,   Lav - en - ders   green.

FOR THE TEACHER

BAR LINES AND MEASURES

The Stave is divided into **bars** or **measures** by **bar lines**. Each measure has an equal number of **beats**. The number **4** at the beginning of the Stave tells us there are four beats to each measure.

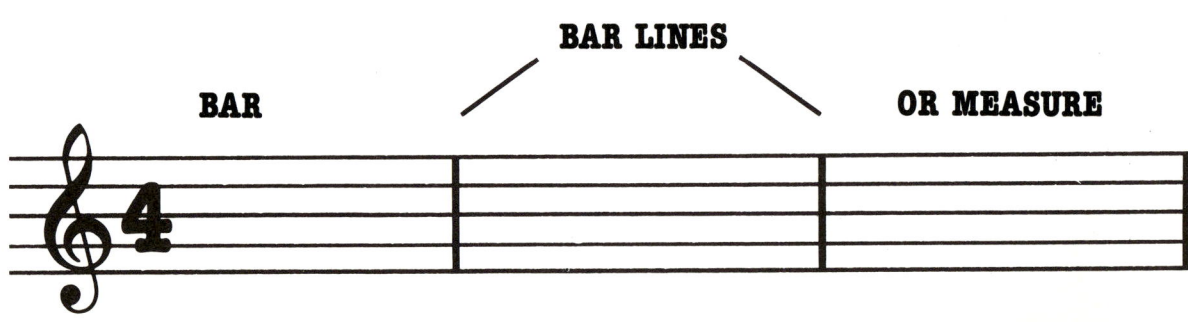

BAR LINES

BAR   OR MEASURE

Tap or clap the four beats to each measure and say the words to this simple song.

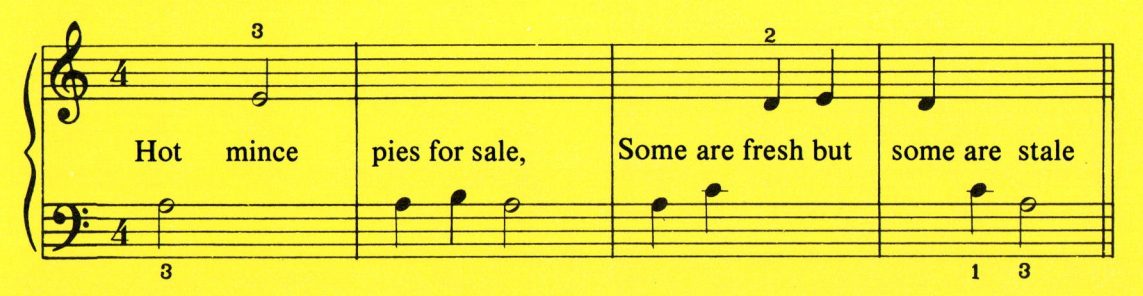

Hot mince | pies for sale, | Some are fresh but | some are stale

Now tap or clap the rhythm of the words and play the song.

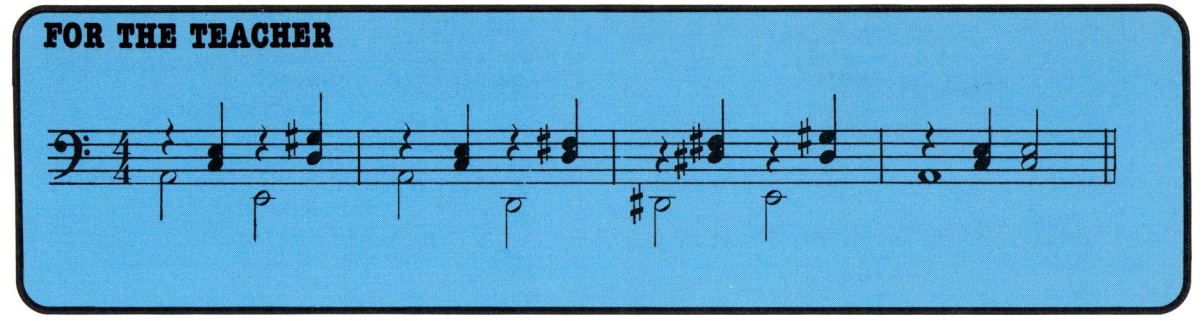

FOR THE TEACHER

CHANGING THE BEAT

We can change the number of beats to the measure.

Try these simple songs, the first with two beats to the measure, and the second with three beats to the measure.

Were you able to play all the tunes correctly? If not, look at page 14 again and practise clapping the beats.

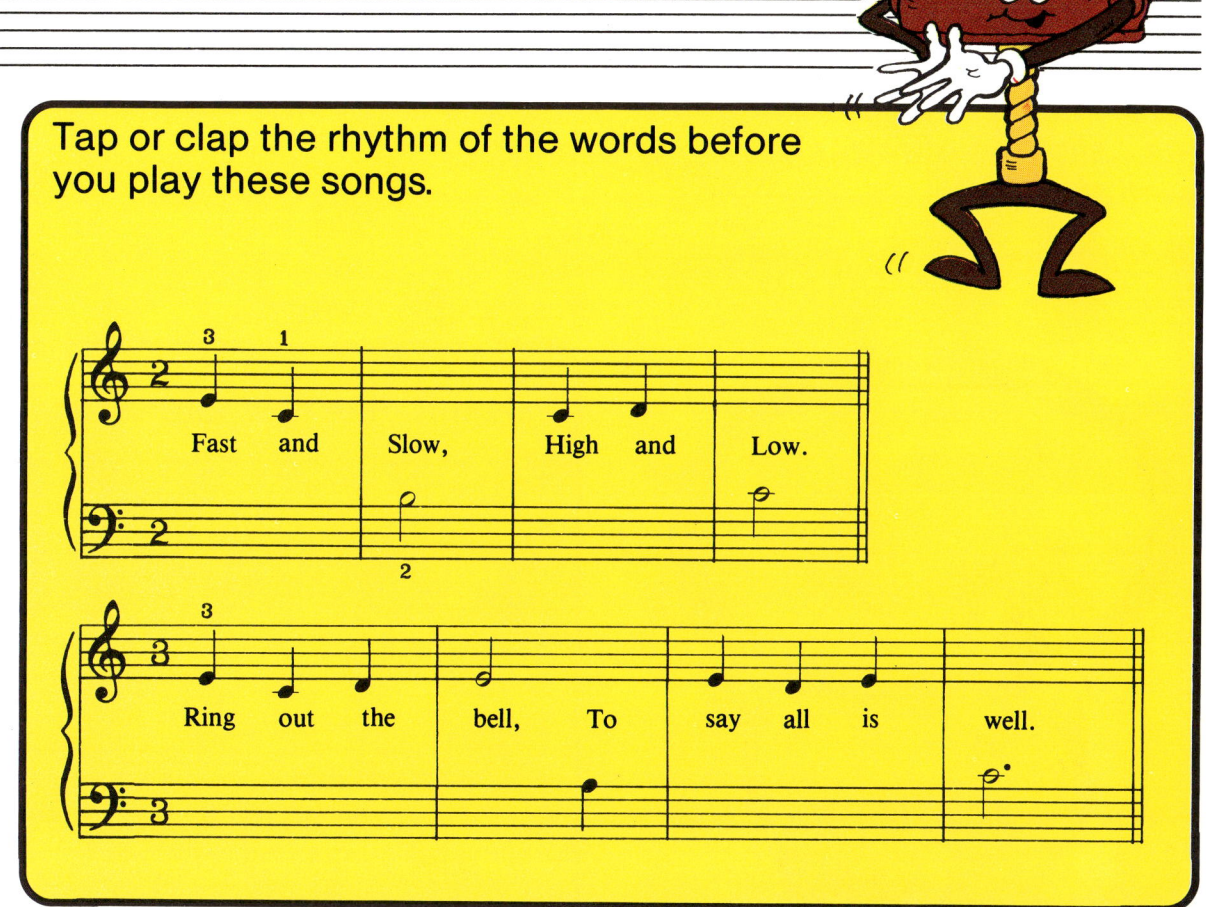

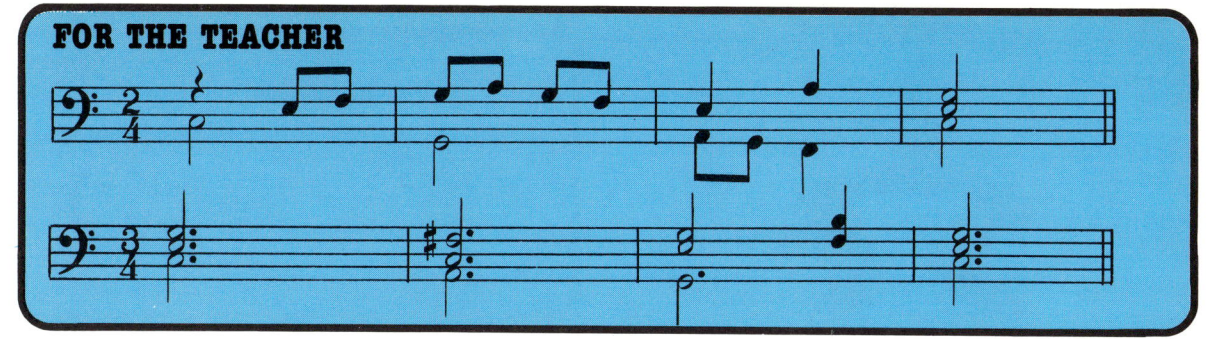

Tap or clap the rhythm of the words before you play these songs.

Fast and Slow, High and Low.

Ring out the bell, To say all is well.

FOR THE TEACHER

WHOLE NOTE – SEMIBREVE

Notes that sound for **four** beats are called **whole notes** or **semibreves**.

A whole note looks like this: 𝅝

A whole note is the longest note of all.

A whole note fills a four beat measure.

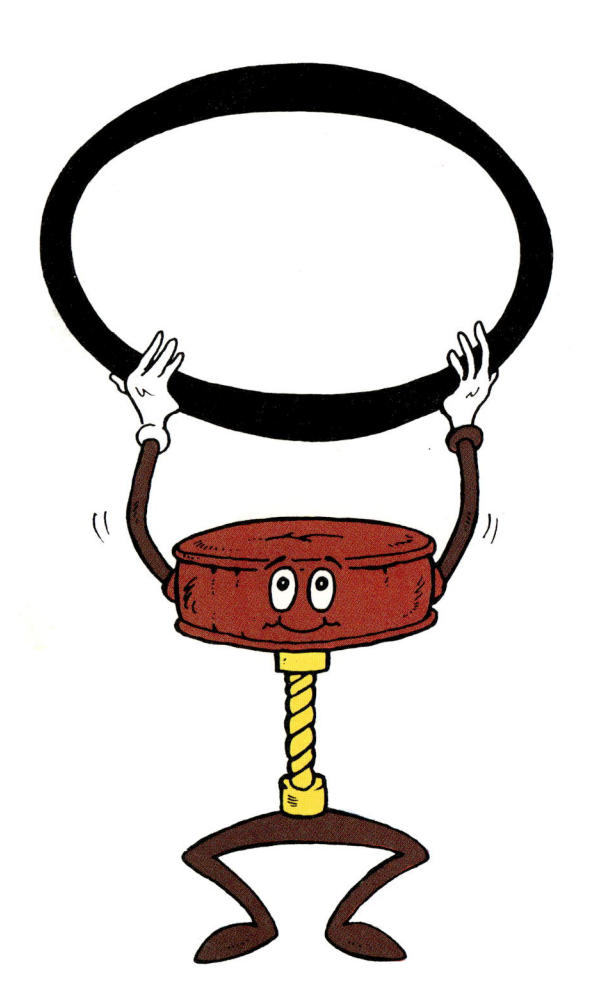

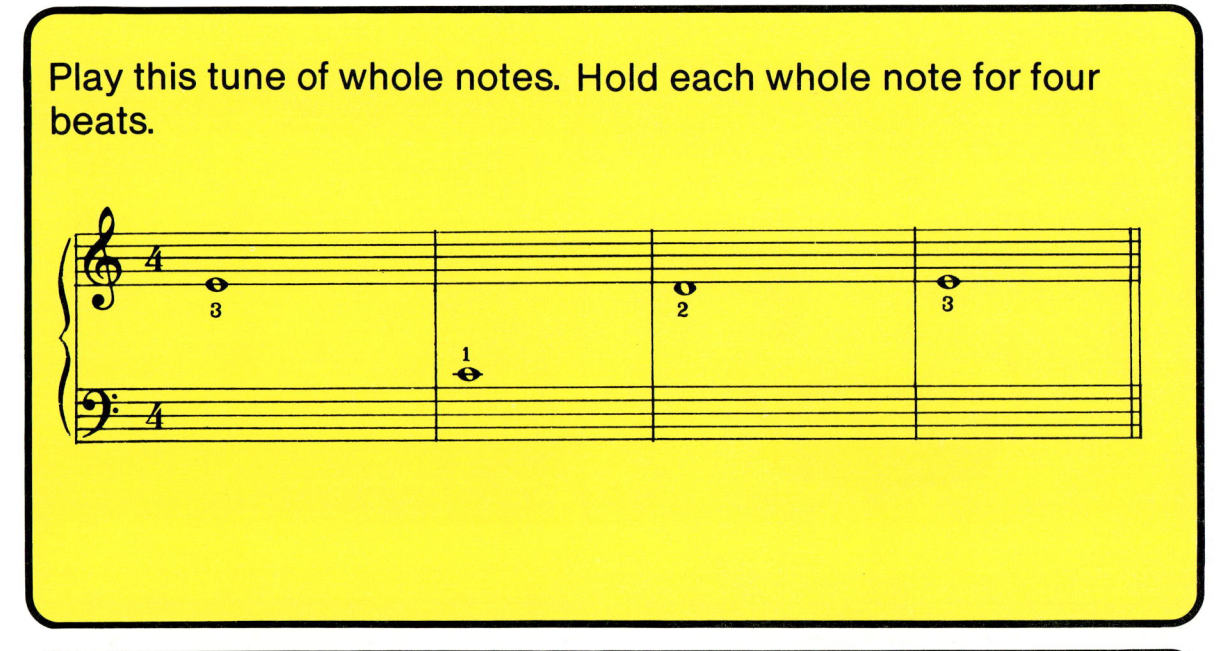

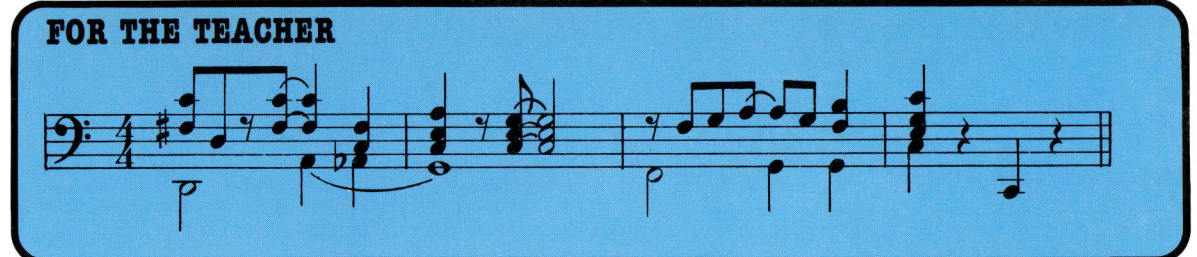

Play this tune of whole notes. Hold each whole note for four beats.

FOR THE TEACHER

HALF NOTE – MINIM

Notes that sound for **two** beats are called **half notes** or **minims**.

A half note looks like this: ♩

A half note has two beats.

Two half notes = one whole note.

♩ + ♩ = 𝅝

Two half notes fill a four beat measure.

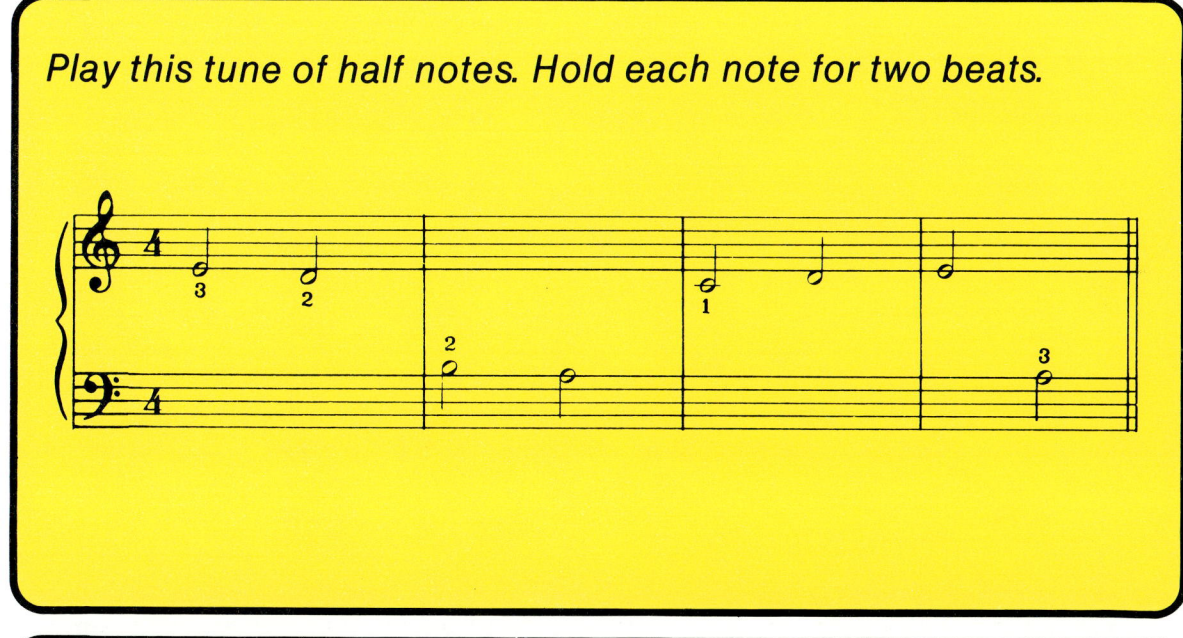

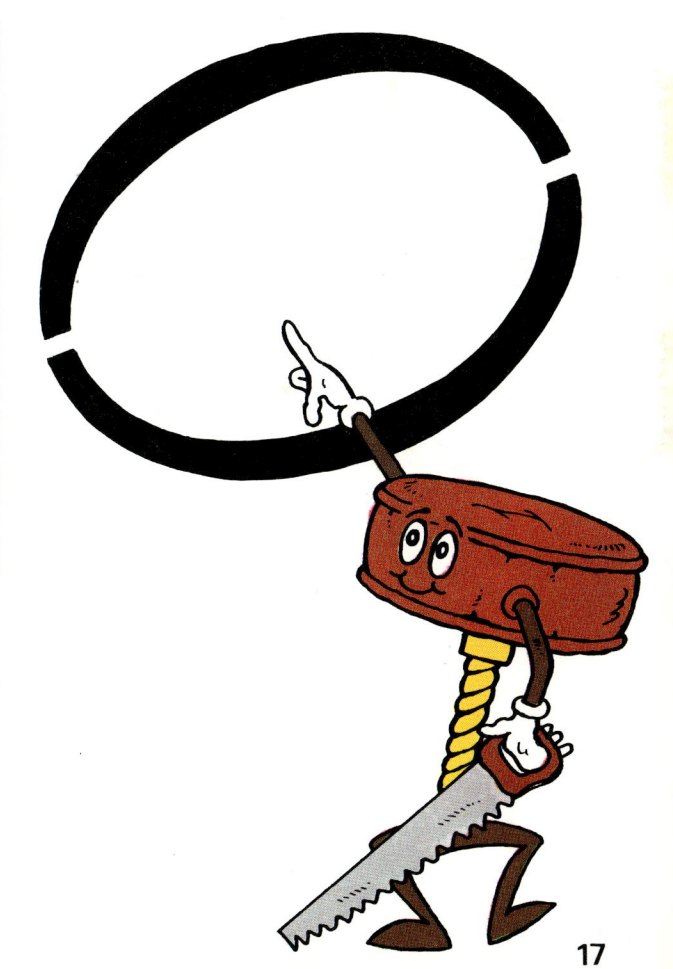

Play this tune of half notes. Hold each note for two beats.

FOR THE TEACHER

QUARTER NOTE CROTCHET

Notes that sound for **one** beat are called **quarter notes** or **crochets.**

Quarter notes look like this: ♩

A quarter note has one beat.

Four quarter notes = one whole note.

♩ + ♩ + ♩ + ♩ = 𝅝

Four quarter notes fill a four beat measure.

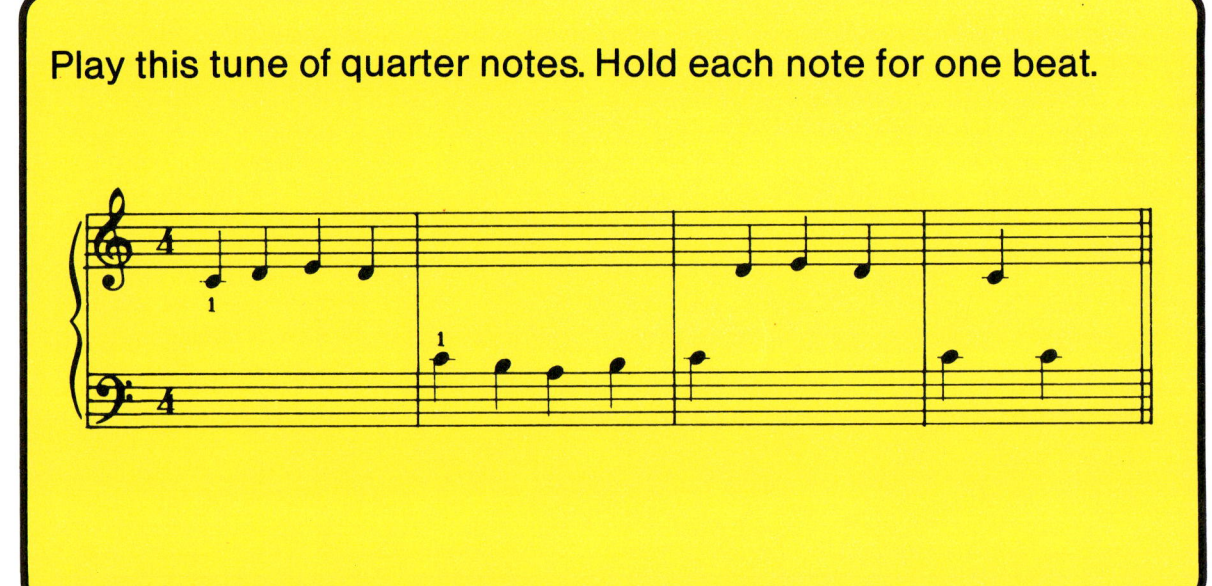

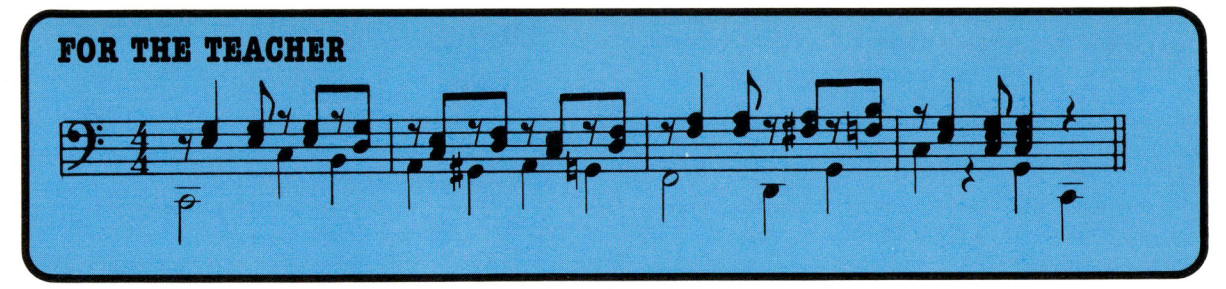

Play this tune of quarter notes. Hold each note for one beat.

FOR THE TEACHER

TUNES TO PLAY

TWO BY TWO

TWO NEW NOTES – LEFT HAND

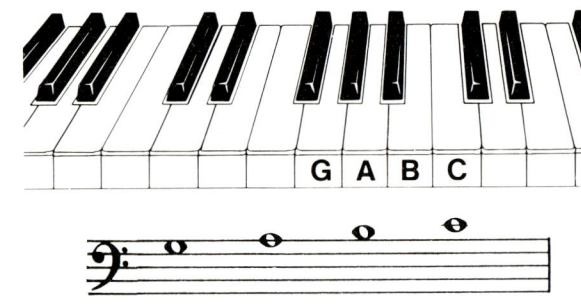

FOR THE TEACHER

One note **lower** than A will be **G**.

G is written in the **top space** of the Bass Clef.

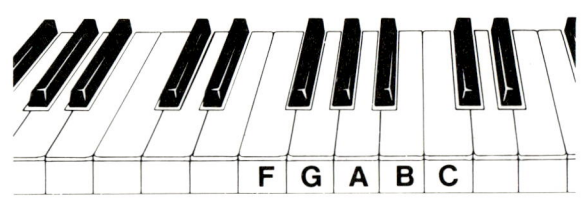

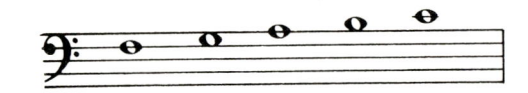

One note **lower** than G will be **F**.

F is written on the **fourth line** of the Bass Clef.

TWO NEW NOTES – RIGHT HAND

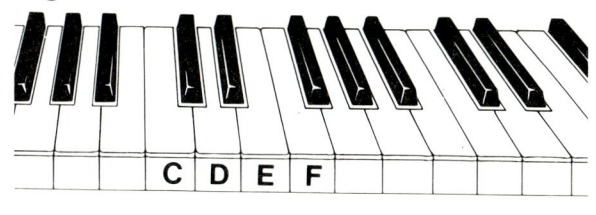

One note **higher** than E is **F**.

F is written in the **first space** of the Treble Clef.

One note **higher** than F will be **G**.

G is written on the **second line** of the Treble Clef.

FOR THE TEACHER

HANDS TOGETHER

When notes are written together on the same beat they should be played together.

THE TIE

A **tie** joins two notes together. Add the two together and play them as **one** long note.

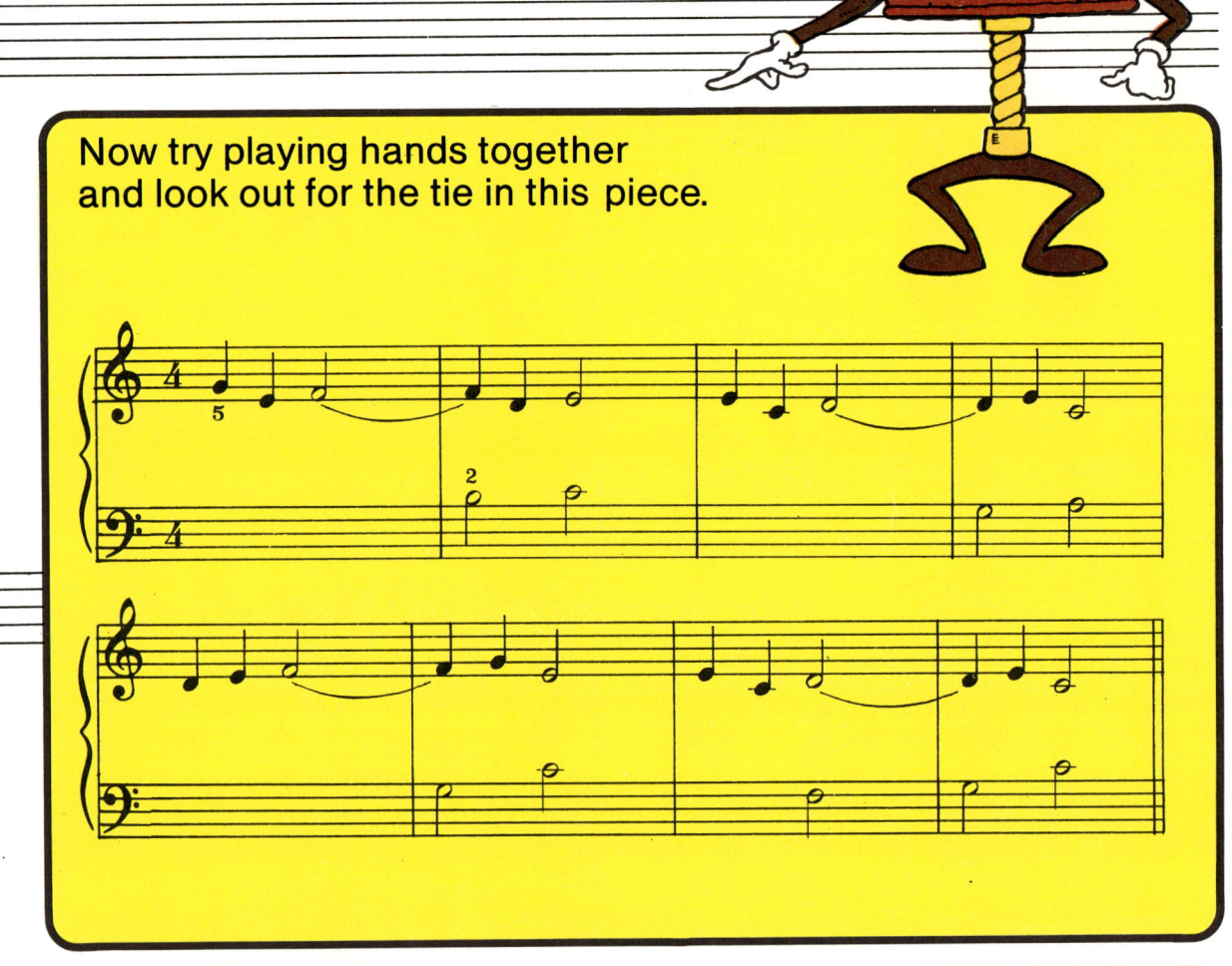

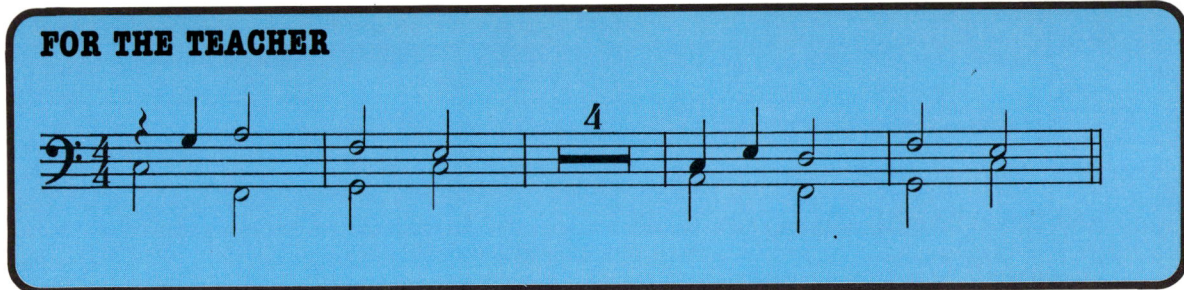

Now try playing hands together and look out for the tie in this piece.

FOR THE TEACHER

DOTTED HALF NOTE

There is another way of writing a three beat note.

A **dot** gives the half note one extra beat.

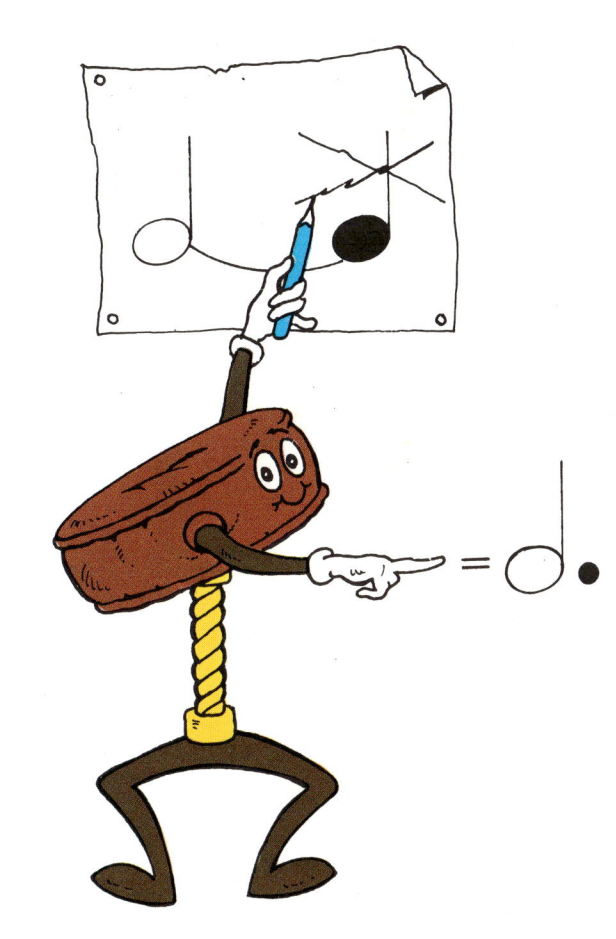

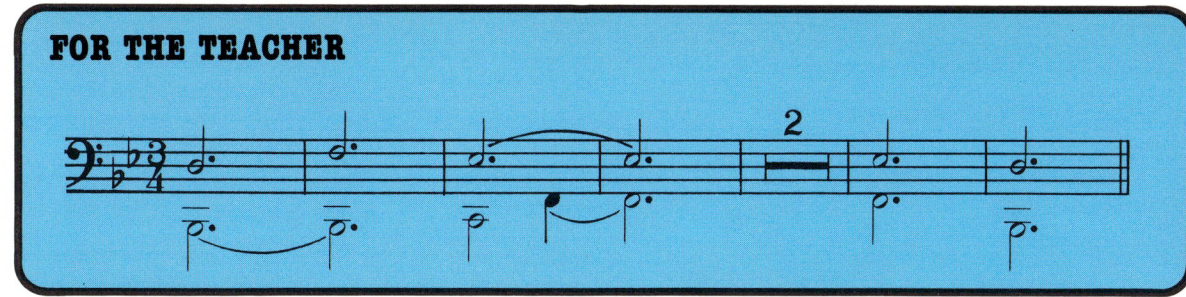

FOR THE TEACHER

EIGHTH NOTE – QUAVER

Notes that sound for half a beat are called **eighth notes** *or* **quavers.**

Eight eighth notes = one whole note.

Eight eighth notes fill a four beat measure.

Eighth notes look like this:

Play this tune of eighth notes.

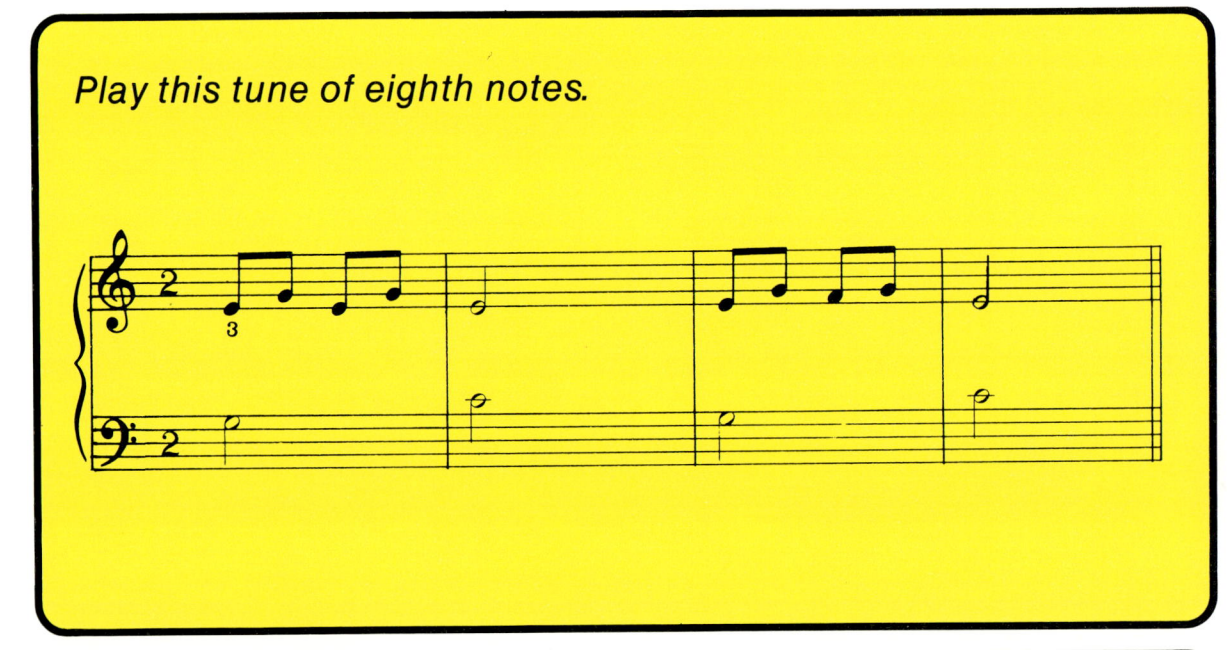

FOR THE TEACHER

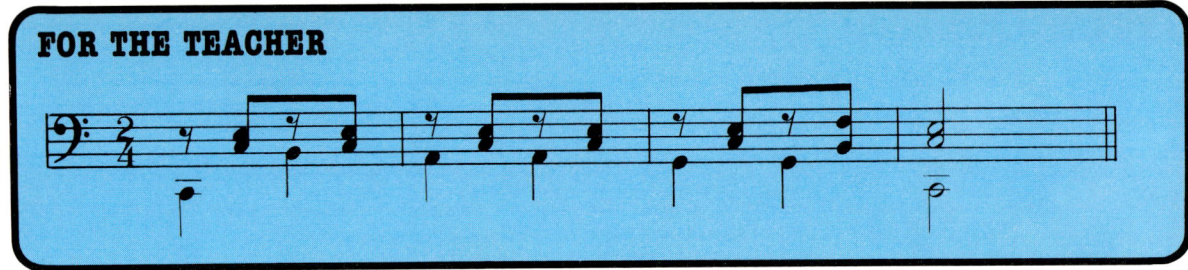

24

TUNES TO PLAY

To make the music more interesting and expressive we sometimes change the sounds and play **loud** and **soft**.

A letter *p* written in the music tells us to play **softly**.

A letter *f* written in the music tells us to play **loudly**.

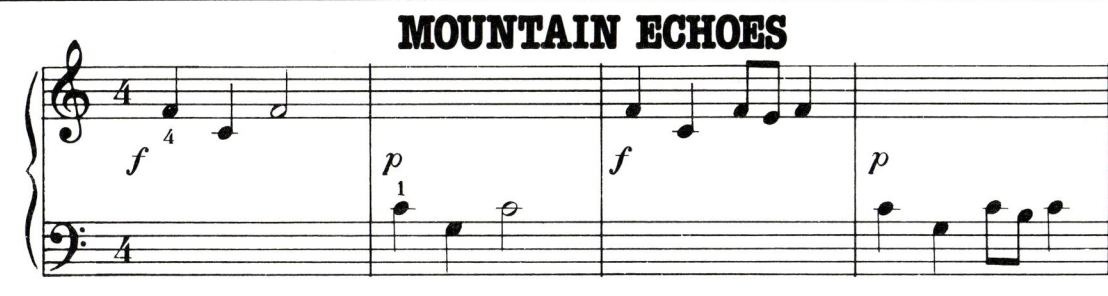

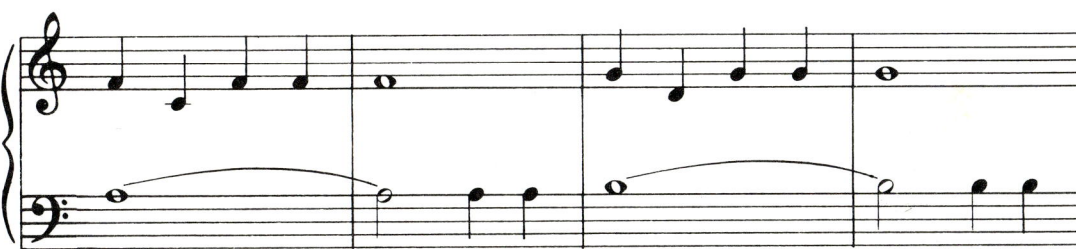

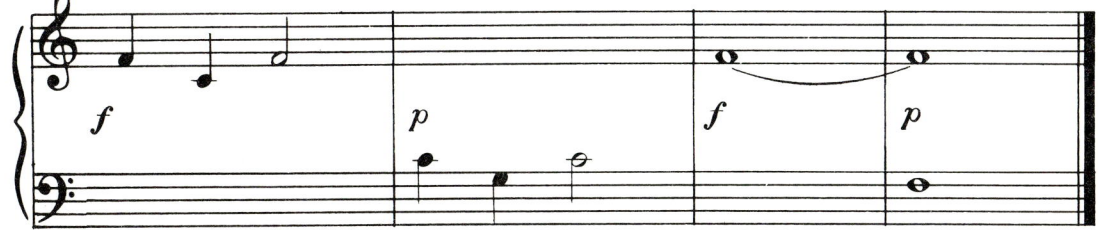

MOUNTAIN ECHOES

To play quietly, press the keys down gently.
To play loudly, press the keys quickly and firmly.

RESTS

Sometimes notes need to rest.

A **rest** tells us when not to play and each note has its own special rest sign.

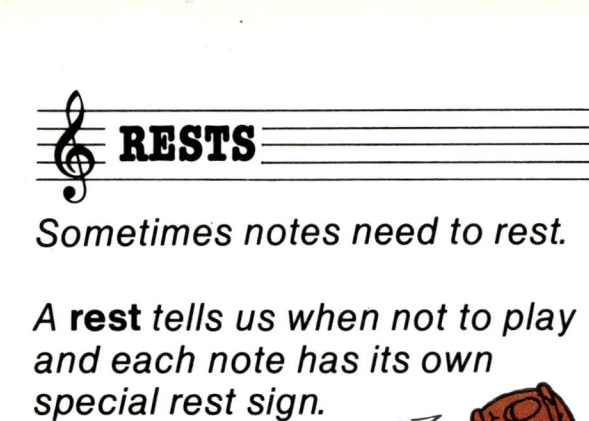

whole note

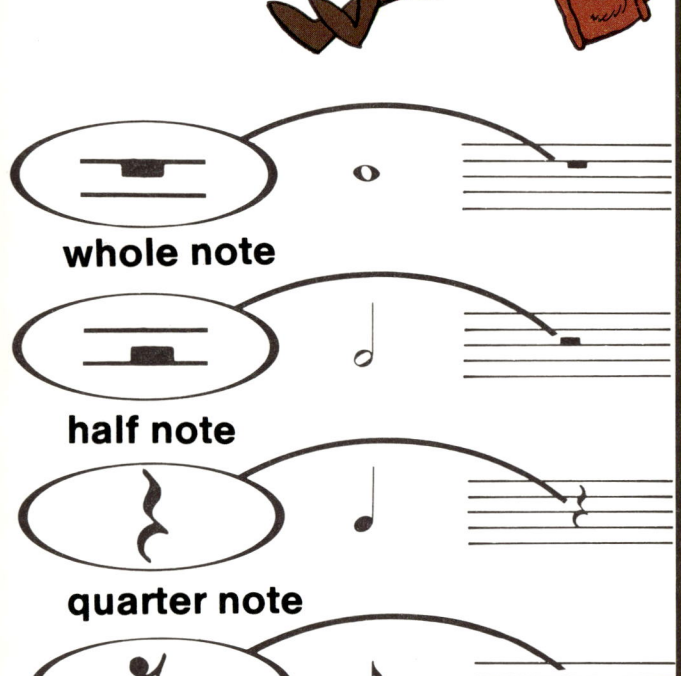

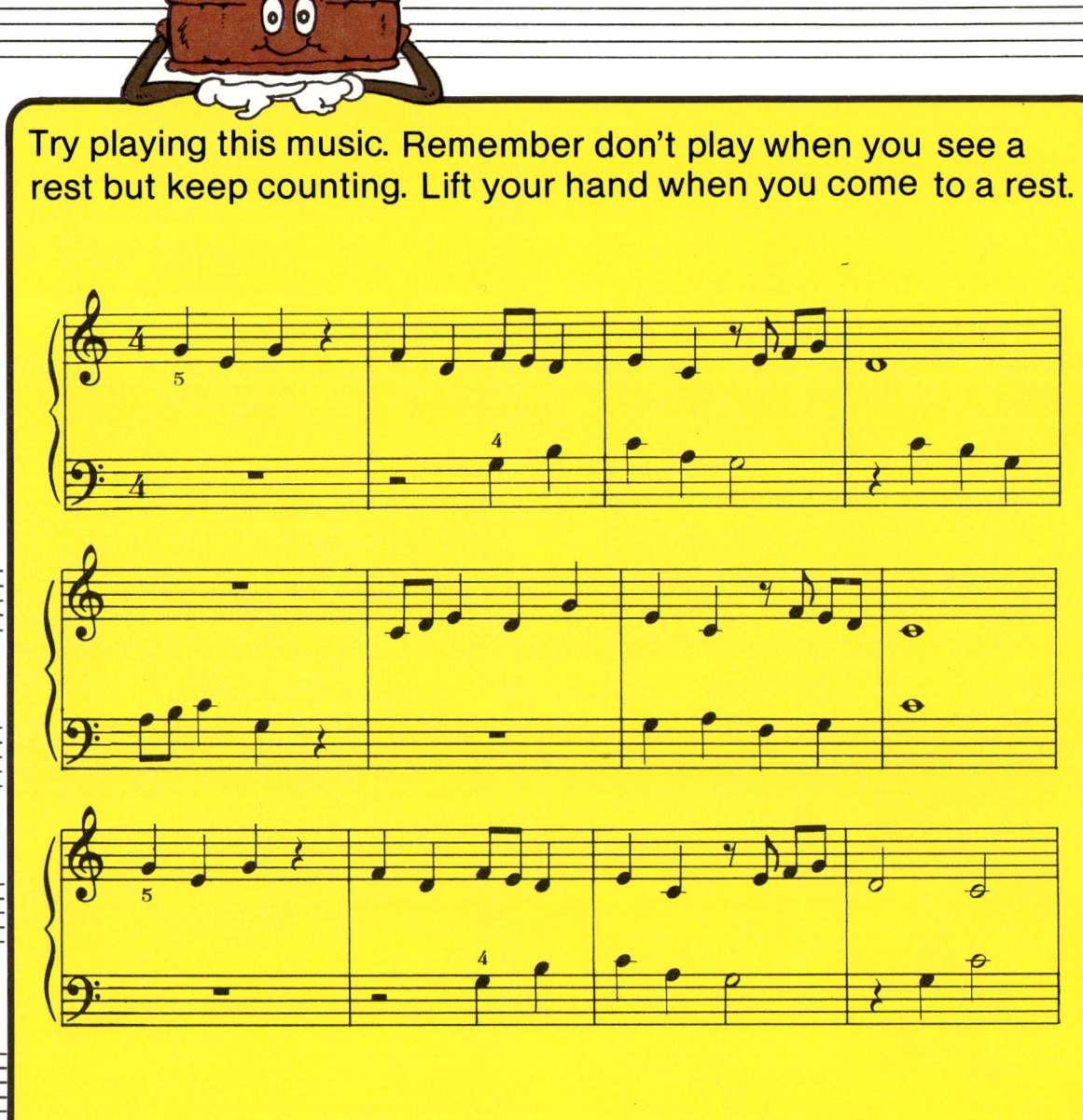

half note

quarter note

eighth note

Try playing this music. Remember don't play when you see a rest but keep counting. Lift your hand when you come to a rest.

TUNES TO PLAY

UP AND DOWN STAIRS

PHRASES

*A **phrase** is a musical sentence. When we speak or sing we join words or notes together in a sentence with one breath.*

Read these words and you'll see what I mean.

Hickory Dickory Dock!
The mouse ran up the clock.

Now sing a few lines from your favourite song. Can you hear the musical sentence? If you stop reading or singing on the wrong word the sentence doesn't make sense.

A sentence in words is shown by a capital letter at the beginning and a full stop at the end.

A musical sentence, or phrase, is shown by a curved line.

Make all the notes in the phrase join together as though you were singing with one breath. At the end of the phrase 'take a breath' by lifting your hand, and then start the next phrase. But remember, don't stop counting.

TUNES TO PLAY

RIDE A SEA HORSE

REPEAT

Play the music between these two signs twice.

These are called **repeat** *signs.*

A NEW NOTE – F SHARP

A **sharp** makes a note a little **higher**.

The sign # in front of a note tells us to play the black key to the right of the white key.

This is **F#** (sharp):

F # (sharp) is the first black key in a group of three. Play all the F#'s on your piano.

Before you begin this piece make sure that the fourth finger of your right hand is covering F#.

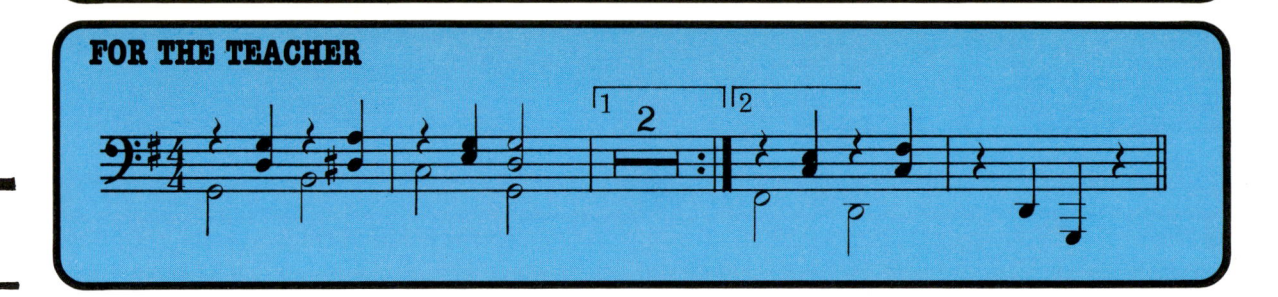

FOR THE TEACHER

TUNES TO PLAY

IN TIME WITH THE BAND

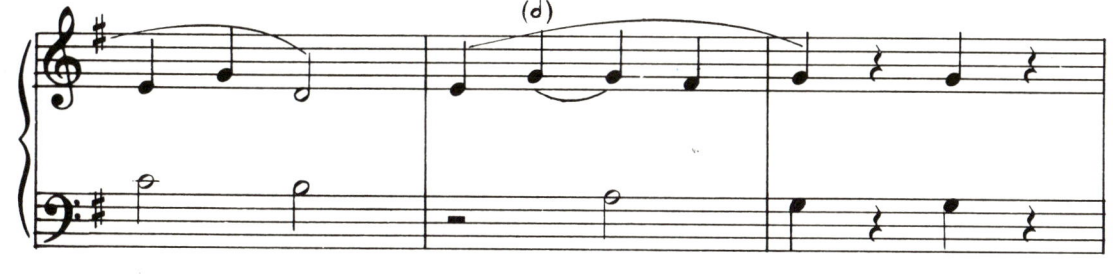

Instead of writing the sharp sign in front of each F it is usually written at the beginning of the Stave. You will find it on the top line in the Treble Clef and on the fourth line in the Bass Clef. This is called the **key signature** and it means that every F will be F#.

A NEW NOTE — B FLAT

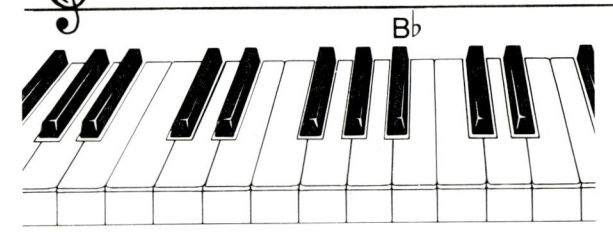

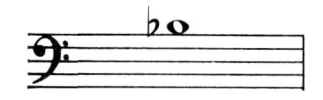

A **flat** makes a note a little **lower**.

The sign ♭ in front of a note tells us to play the black key to the left of the white key.

B♭ (flat) is the top black key in a group of three. Play all the B♭'s on your piano.

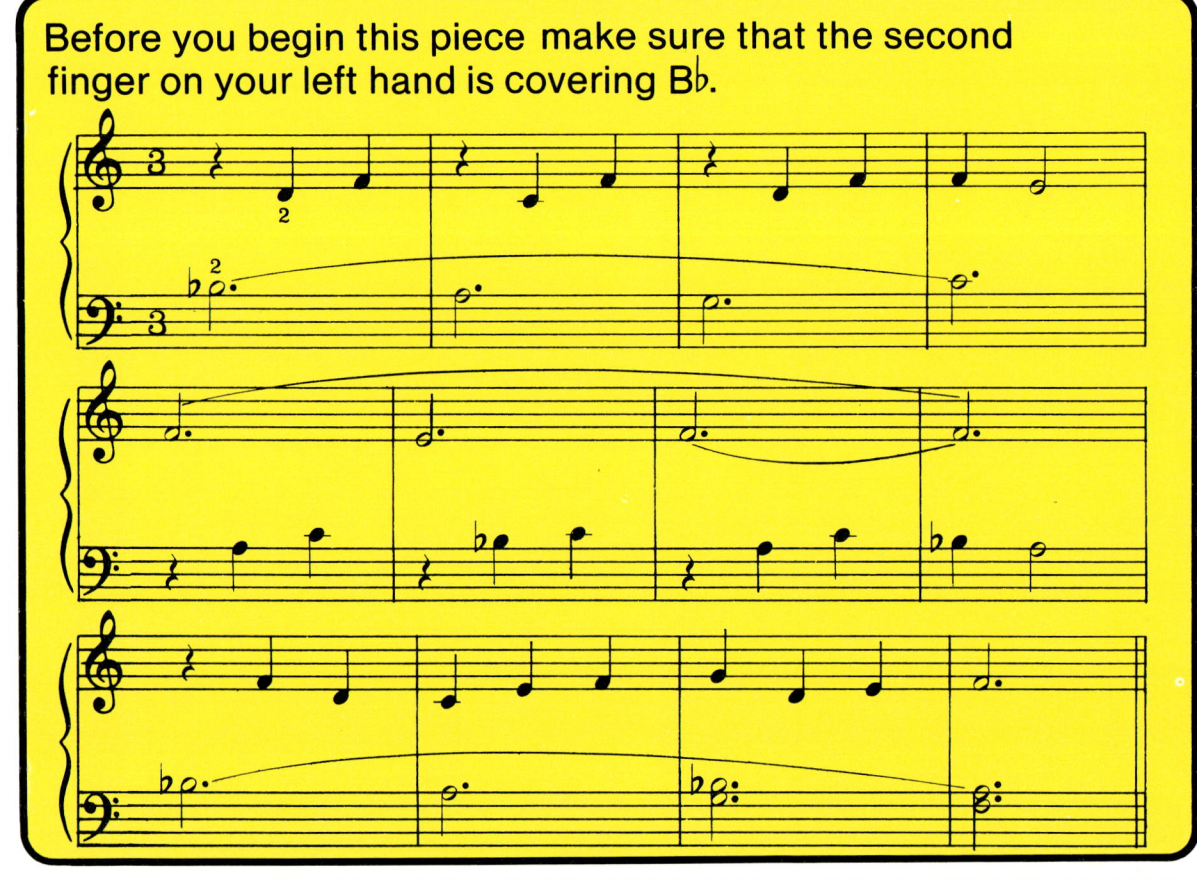

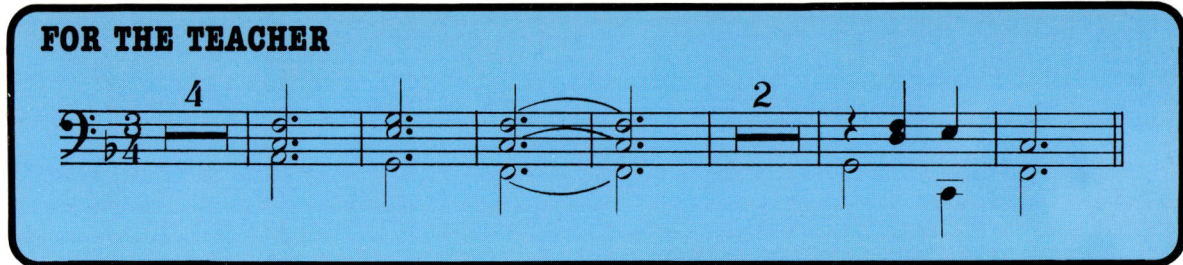

Before you begin this piece make sure that the second finger on your left hand is covering B♭.

FOR THE TEACHER

TUNES TO PLAY

JUMPING ON THE MOON

Instead of writing the flat sign in front of each B it is usually written at the beginning of the Stave. You will find it on the second line in the Bass Clef, and on the third line in the Treble Clef. Every B will be B♭.

TIME FOR MUSIC

At the beginning of most music you will see two numbers. These are called the **time signature.**

The top number tells us how many beats there are in a measure.

The bottom number tells us the note value of each beat.

The 4/4 time signature tells us there are four beats in a measure and each beat is the value of a quarter note.

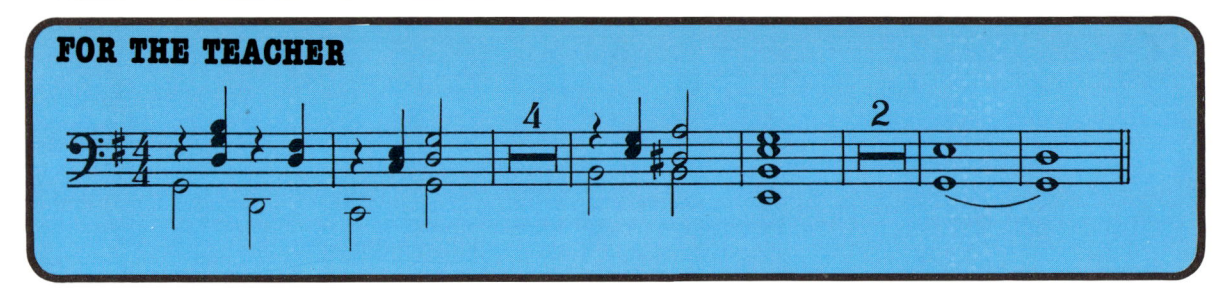

FOR THE TEACHER

TUNES TO PLAY

THE SINGING SEAL

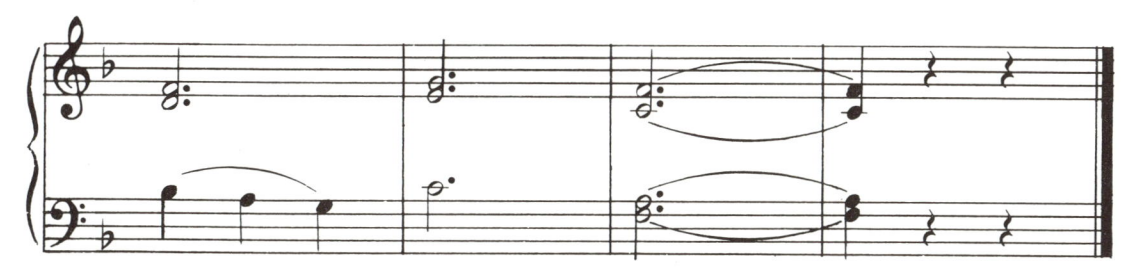

The $\frac{3}{4}$ time signature tells us there are three beats in a measure, and each beat is the value of a quarter note.

MORE NEW NOTES – LEFT HAND

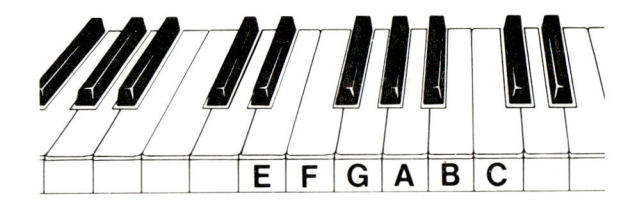

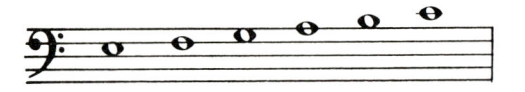

To play the new note **E** in the Bass Clef, we have to move the position of the left hand.

Look carefully at the finger numbers underneath the notes.

To play E in the next piece move the 5th finger down one note from F to E when the note appears.

MORE NEW NOTES – RIGHT HAND

To play the new note **A** in the Treble Clef we have to move the position of the right hand.

Look carefully at the finger numbers over the notes.

To play A in the next piece move the 5th finger up one note from G to A when the note appears.

TUNES TO PLAY

THE PAUSE

When you see this sign over a note, stop counting and hold the note for as long as you like.

Look out for the pause in these tunes.

SHORT STEPS, LONG STEPS

TUNES TO PLAY

LITTLE LOST SPACEMAN

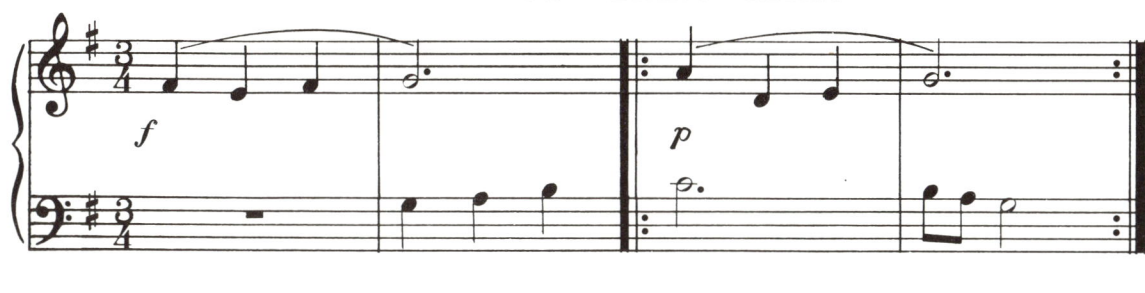

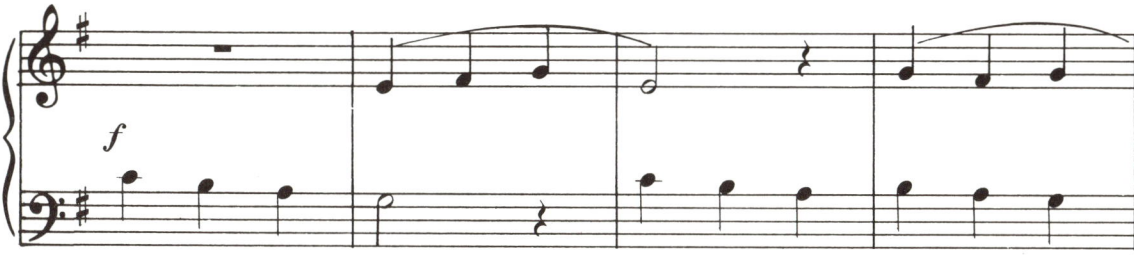

PLAYING A SCALE — LEFT HAND

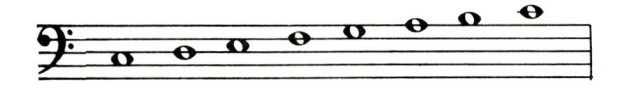

Now you can play all the notes in the Bass Clef from C-C but in order to do that you have to **cross your fingers**.

Put your first finger on C and play C B A. Now cross your first finger under your hand to play G, and go straight down.

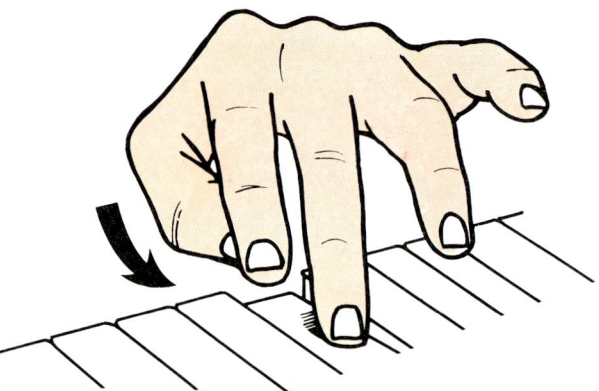

Scale is from a Latin word which means ladder, and playing like this is like coming down a ladder.

TUNES TO PLAY

AS SLOW AS A SNAIL

PLAYING A SCALE – RIGHT HAND

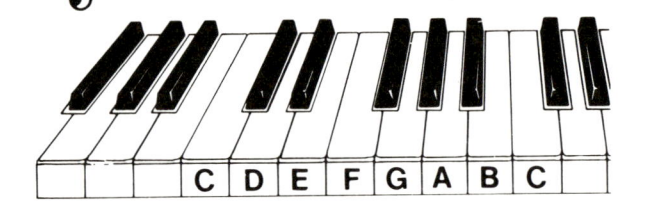

Now you can play all the notes in the Treble Clef from C-C and again you have to **cross your fingers**.

Put your first finger on C and play C D E.

Now cross your first finger under your hand to play F, then go straight up to top C.

When you play all the notes from C – C like this it is called playing a **SCALE**.

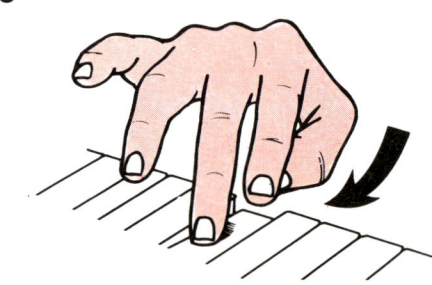

Now you are walking up the ladder.

TUNES TO PLAY

SPLASHING IN THE RAIN

TUNES TO PLAY

STACCATO

When you see a **dot** under or over a note play it short and crisp, but don't hurry the beat.

Playing like this is called **staccato.**

CRAZY COMPUTER

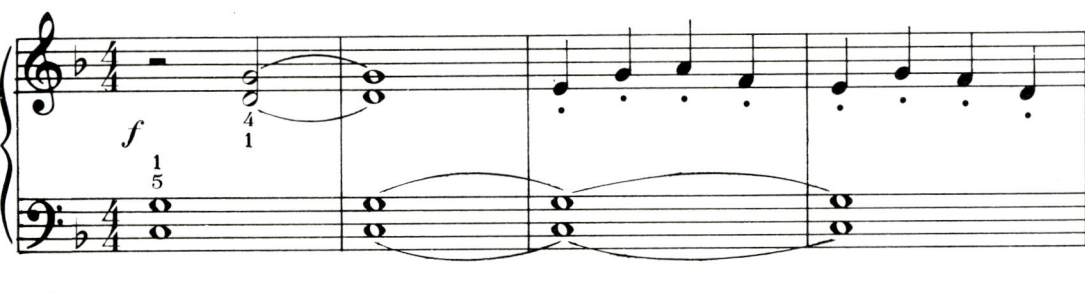

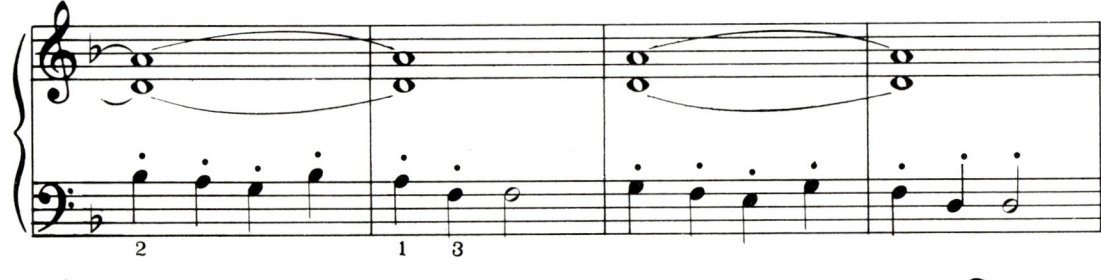

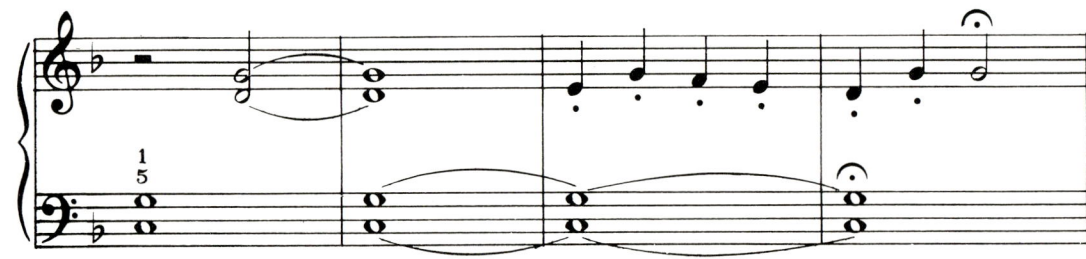

TUNES TO PLAY

ELEPHANTS WALK

TUNES TO PLAY

DOTTED QUARTER NOTE

A dot makes a quarter note half a beat longer. ♩. = ♩ + ♪

COUNTING SHEEP

TUNES TO PLAY

MELTING SNOWMAN

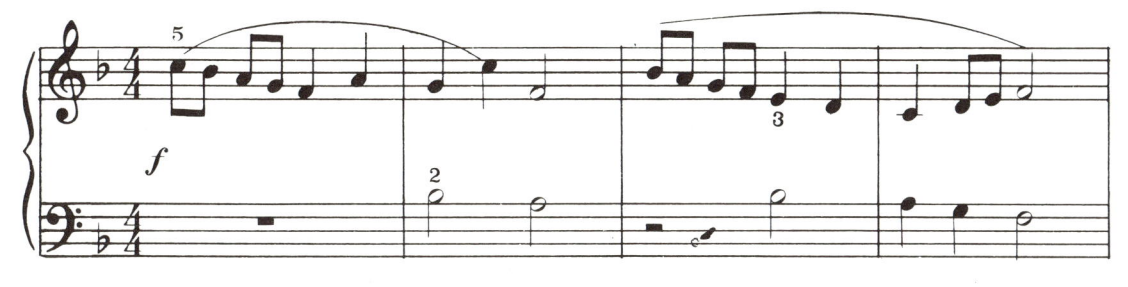

TUNES TO PLAY

ROBOT'S BALL

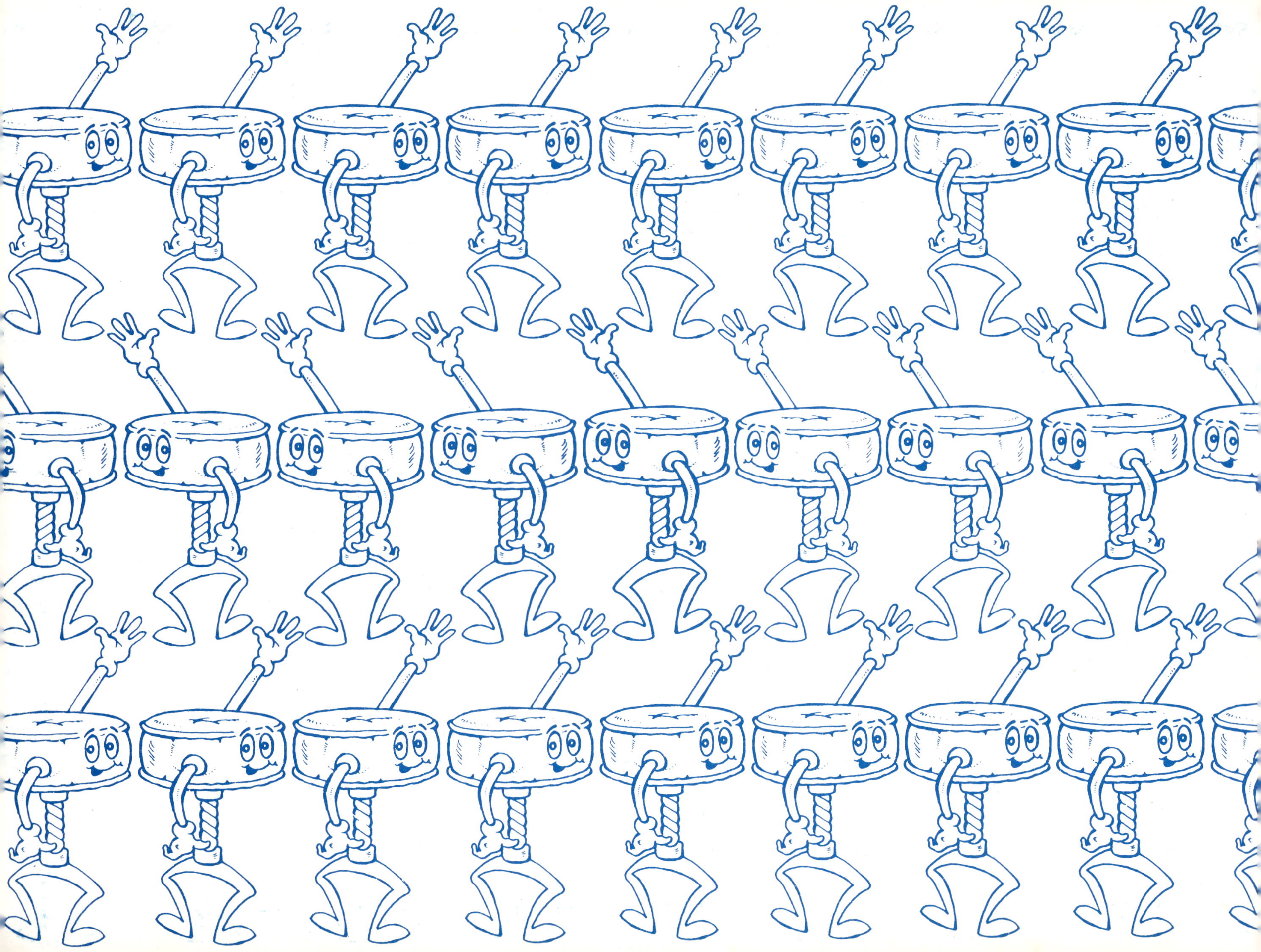